THE
NEW
SUPERVISOR

Elwood N. Chapman

CRISP PUBLICATIONS, INC.
Los Altos, California

THE NEW SUPERVISOR

(Previously published as The Fifty-Minute Supervisor)

by Elwood N. Chapman

CREDITS
Editor: **Michael Crisp**
Designer: **Carol Harris**
Layout and Composition: **Interface Studio**
Cover Design: **Carol Harris**

Copyright © 1986, 1988, 1992 by Crisp Publications, Inc.
Printed in the United States of America

English language Crisp books are distributed worldwide. Our major international distributors include:

CANADA: Reid Publishing, Ltd., Box 69559—109 Thomas St., Oakville, Ontario Canada L6J 7R4. TEL: (416) 842-4428, FAX: (416) 842-9327

AUSTRALIA: Career Builders, P. O. Box 1051, Springwood, Brisbane, Queensland, Australia 4127. TEL: 841-1061, FAX: 841-1580

NEW ZEALAND: Career Builders, P. O. Box 571, Manurewa, Auckland, New Zealand. TEL: 266-5276, FAX: 266-4152

JAPAN: Phoenix Associates Co., Mizuho Bldg. 2-12-2, Kami Osaki, Shinagawa-Ku, Tokyo 141, Japan. TEL: 3-443-7231, FAX: 3-443-7640

Selected Crisp titles are also available in other languages. Contact International Rights Manager Tim Polk at (415) 949-4888 for more information.

Library of Congress Cataloging in Publication Data 91-77082
Chapman, Elwood N.
The New Supervisor
ISBN 1-56052-120-1

PREFACE

Improving the quality of first line supervision has always been considered essential by successful organizations because of the immediate impact on employee productivity. As a result, many companies allocate a sizable portion of their budget to new supervisor training. A common problem, however, has been that considerable time may elapse between the time a new supervisor is promoted and before formal training is provided. This can lead to costly mistakes or the formation of poor habits before training takes place. *The New Supervisor* was developed to remedy this "training dealy" problem.

The New Supervisor should be considered Phase I of any training program. It was primarily designed as a helpful resource to be given to a new supervisor or an acting supervisor as soon as practical following promotion.

To complete the *New Supervisor* program, all that is required is a pencil, a chair and some time. Once completed this program should help a new supervisor get off to a successful start. Later, following an on-the-job adjustment period, the individual will be better prepared for Phase II — a more formal supervisory training program.

For a group program, *The New Supervisor* video is available from the publisher. It was developed around this book and is available for preview by writing Crisp Publications, Inc., 95 First Street, Los Altos, California 94022 or calling (415) 949-4888.

Earlier editions of this book appeared under the title of *The Fifty-Minute Supervisor*. Thanks to all who made suggestions for its improvement.

ABOUT THIS BOOK

The New Supervisor is not like most books. It has a unique self-paced format that encourages a reader to become personally involved. Designed to be read-with-a-pencil, there is an abundance of exercises, activities, assessments and cases that invite participation.

The objective of this book is to help a person recognize the traits that lead to successful supervision and then make any required behavioral changes that apply the concepts presented in the book.

The New Supervisor can be used effectively in a number of ways. Here are some possibilities:

— **Individual Study.** Because the book is self-instructional, it can be introduced at the point of promotion. By completing the activities and exercises, a person should receive not only valuable feedback, but also practical ideas about steps for self-improvement.

— **Workshops and Seminars.** The book, along with the *New Supervisor* video, is ideal for a workshop or seminar. The book can also be effective as a self-study reference.

— **Remote Location Training.** Copies of both book and video can be sent to those not able to attend ''home office'' training sessions. The complete *New Supervisor* video/book program is ideal for organizations that have a large number of remote offices.

— **Informal Study Groups.** Thanks to the format, brevity and low cost, this book is ideal for brown-bag or other informal group sessions.

There are other possibilities that depend on the objectives, program or ideas or the user. As you will soon learn, it is a hands-on approach to learning the basics of supervision.

TO THE READER

Congratulations on becoming a supervisor. After completing this brief book you will know many secrets of good supervision. Any positive changes you make in your behavior, are far more important than the time it takes to finish, so please *do not read so fast that you miss something.*

To fully benefit, be honest, especially when you rate yourself on factors such as attitude and self-confidence. It is not what you are now, but what you can become as a successful supervisor that will help you progress in your organization. Good luck in your new venture.

Elwood N. Chapman

Elwood N. Chapman

P.S. The person who gave you this believes in your future. If you have a problem as you proceed, please return to this individual for assistance. Keep this guide as a resource and refer to it on a regular basis as you make your transition into management.

Many new, inexperienced supervisors enjoy setting success goals for themselves. A good way to do this is to identify, discuss, and refine such goals with your immediate superior and then ask this person to monitor your progress for a thirty-day period. If you wish, you can formalize this process by using the Voluntary Contract on the opposite page. One advantage in using the agreement is that your superior will recognize your sincerity and set a firm date for a review. Using the contract approach is a form of self-motivation.

VOLUNTARY
CONTRACT

I, _____ , hereby agree

(Your name)

to meet with the individual designated below within

thirty days to discuss my progress toward incorporating

the techniques and ideas presented in this supervisory

training program. The purpose of this meeting will be

to *review* areas of strength and establish action steps for

areas where improvement may still be required.

_____

Signature

I agree to meet with the above employee on,

_____

Month   *Date*   *Time*

at the following location.

_____

_____

Signature

CONTENTS

PART I

DEVELOPING A MANAGERIAL ATTITUDE

Attitude is the way you look at things *mentally.* You have the power to look at your new position in any way you wish. If you look at it in a positive, enthusiastic manner you will communicate to your employees that you are *ready* to accept your new responsibility and they will enjoy working for you. If you are tentative or insecure they may interpret your attitude as negative and you may receive less cooperation.

As a new supervisor, everyone will be watching you, and no matter what you may do to hide it, your attitude will be showing.

YOUR ATTITUDE TOWARD BEING A SUPERVISOR

To measure your attitude, please complete this exercise. Read the statement and circle the number where you feel you belong. If you circle a 5, you are saying your attitude could not be better in this area; if you circle a 1, you are saying supervision may not be for you.

	Agree				Disagree
I seek responsibility.	5	4	3	2	1
Becoming a respected supervisor is important to me.	5	4	3	2	1
I enjoy helping others do a good job.	5	4	3	2	1
I want to know more about human behavior.	5	4	3	2	1
I want to climb the management ladder.	5	4	3	2	1
I am anxious to learn and master supervisory skills.	5	4	3	2	1
I like leadership situations.	5	4	3	2	1
Working with a problem employee would be an interesting challenge.	5	4	3	2	1
I intend to devote time to learn motivational skills.	5	4	3	2	1
I'm excited about the opportunity to become a supervisor.	5	4	3	2	1

TOTAL

If you scored above 40, you have an excellent attitude toward becoming a supervisor. If you rated yourself between 25 and 40, it would appear you have a few reservations. A rating under 25 indicates you probably should not pursue becoming a supervisor.

ATTITUDE AND PRODUCTIVITY

Nothing will improve relationships with those you supervise more than a consistently positive attitude on your part. Your attitude sets the pace and the tone in your department. If you are late to work, it will be reflected in the attitudes of your employees. If you complain about work conditions, it will impact in a negative way on their attitudes. Everything you do and every position you take will be reflected in the attitudes of your employees. Two expressions are appropriate. They are:

> **1. ATTITUDES ARE CAUGHT, NOT TAUGHT!**
>
> **2. YOUR ATTITUDE SPEAKS SO LOUDLY, EMPLOYEES CAN'T HEAR WHAT YOU SAY.**

There is a direct relationship between your attitude and the productivity of those you supervise. When you are upbeat, your employees will respond in positive ways that will enhance productivity. When you are negative, a drop in productivity can be expected.

PRODUCTIVITY GAPS

In the diagram below, you will notice that there is a gap between what a hypothetical *department* is producing and what it *could* produce. We call this a departmental productivity gap. You will also notice there is a gap between what the *employees* are producing and what they *could* produce. Such gaps are normal and to be expected.

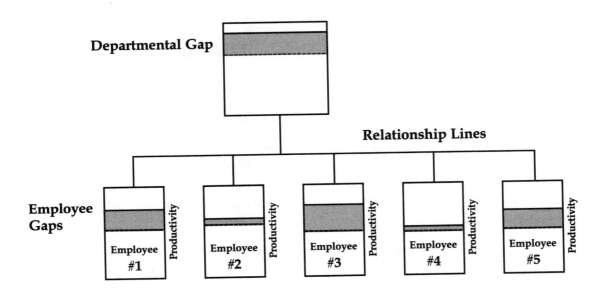

So how do you close the departmental productivity gap? The answer is to build such good relationships with your employees that they are motivated to close their individual productivity gaps. Of course, as a working supervisor, what you produce yourself is important. But it is the sum total of all producers that narrows the departmental gap, not what you can do yourself.

All successful managers will tell you that it is what others produce for you that makes the difference. It is a lesson some beginning supervisors fail to learn.

THE CHALLENGE AHEAD

Supervision is a special challenge that can help you reach new career and lifestyle goals. But becoming a successful manager is not as easy as some people imagine. Three factors will require that you be a different kind of person on the job.

1. Those in your department will expect you to lead where in the past you have been, like them, a follower. This means they will be watching your actions in the hope that you will make quick and good decisions that will lead the department in the direction that is best for the organization.

2. Your new role will put you in the position of being a buffer between your superiors and those you supervise. This means you must satisfy your superiors and, at the same time, keep your employees happy so they will maintain high productivity. At times this may mean it is best for you to absorb pressure from above rather than pass it on to your employees.

3. You will be setting standards rather than living up to those set by others. This means you will be responsible for creating a disciplined environment where employees do not violate company standards as well as those set by you. When violations occur, some sensitive counseling on your part may be necessary.

All of this should be accepted as a challenge that will help you grow into a stronger person. And, of course, there are special rewards as listed on the next page.

WHAT CAN SUCCESS AS A SUPERVISOR DO FOR YOU?

Many good things can happen to you once you become a successful supervisor. Ten statements are listed below. *Three are false.* Place a check in the square opposite these false statements and match your answers with those at the bottom of the page.

As a supervisor you will:

☐ 1. Increase your earnings potential.
☐ 2. Have opportunities to learn more.
☐ 3. Develop an ulcer.
☐ 4. Position yourself for promotions to higher management.
☐ 5. Have less freedom.
☐ 6. Increase your self-confidence.
☐ 7. Try out your leadership wings.
☐ 8. Have fewer friends.
☐ 9. Learn and develop human relations skills.
☐ 10. Have better feelings of self-worth.

You will find the answers to this exercise at the bottom of the page.

FALSE STATEMENTS

3. There is no evidence that supervisors have more ulcers than non-supervisors.
5. Supervisors normally have more freedom because they control their actions more than employees.
8. Good supervisors develop new friends (fellow supervisors) and keep many old ones.

As you contemplate making your transition into a supervisory role, it is often a good idea to model your behavior after a successful supervisor you respect.

You will discover that the highly successful supervisors have much in common. If the opportunity presents itself, discuss some of the characteristics and principles of good supervision with your manager. Some of these characteristics are presented on the next page.

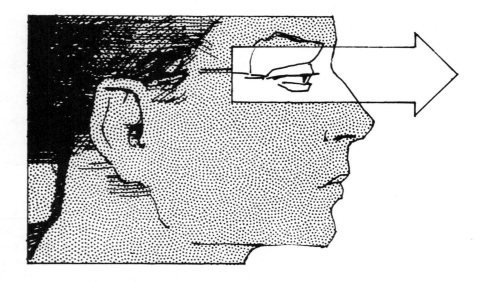

MAKE YOUR CHOICE NOW

SUCCESSFUL SUPERVISORS

Supervisors who remain positive under stress.

Those who take time to teach employees what they know.

Those who build and maintain mutually rewarding relationships with their employees.

Supervisors who learn to set reasonable and consistent authority lines.

Those who learn to delegate.

Those who establish standards of high quality and set good examples.

Individuals who work hard to become good communicators.

Leaders who build team effort to achieve high productivity.

FAILURES

Supervisors who permit problems to get them down.

Those who rush instructions to employees and then fail to follow up.

Individuals insensitive to employee needs.

Those not interested in learning the basic supervisory skills.

Those who fail to understand that it is not what a *supervisor* can do, but what supervisors can get *others* to accomplish.

Supervisors who let their status go to their heads.

Those who become either too authoritarian or too lax.

Add your own:

_____   _____

_____   _____

_____   _____

As an employee, you have had the opportunity to study mistakes supervisors make. List three you do not intend to make.

1. _____

2. _____

3. _____

Along with a positive attitude, it takes personal confidence to become a successful supervisor. When you first start out, you may not have *all* the confidence you would like, *but do not lose faith in yourself.* As a supervisor, you will slowly build your level of personal confidence. That is one of the advantages in becoming a supervisor in the first place.

As you accomplish this goal, keep in mind that you need not be a highly verbal extrovert to be successful. Quiet, sensitive people become excellent supervisors even though they may not show their personal confidence on the outside.

You have the ''right stuff'' or your superiors would not have given you the opportunity to become a supervisor in the first place. In management circles, the ''potted plant'' theory is often expressed. Sometimes, like a plant that is root-bound in a pot that is too small to permit growth, an employee often out-grows his or her position and only through a promotion into greater responsibilities (larger pot) can growth continue. This may be the best way to view your move into a supervisory role.

SELF-CONFIDENCE SCALE

This exercise is designed to help you discover your level of self-confidence. Read the statement and circle the number where you feel you belong.

	Agree				Disagree
I'm not easily intimidated.	5	4	3	2	1
Complex problems do not overwhelm me.	5	4	3	2	1
If necessary, I can discipline those who require it.	5	4	3	2	1
I can make a decision and stick with it.	5	4	3	2	1
I am strong enough to defend a deserving employee with a superior.	5	4	3	2	1
I have enough confidence to be a good teacher.	5	4	3	2	1
Speaking in public does not frighten me.	5	4	3	2	1
Superiors are basically people like me.	5	4	3	2	1
I won't avoid confrontations when required.	5	4	3	2	1
I can say ''no'' when necessary.	5	4	3	2	1

TOTAL

If you scored 40 or above on both attitude and self-confidence, you have a winning combination as far as being a successful supervisor is concerned. If you scored lower on self-confidence than attitude, it is a signal that you need to learn to take a firmer stand on those items relating to supervision.

A case study is designed to provide insights you may not possess. Five case problems are included in this program. Please give them your careful attention.

The case on the opposite page will help you understand some of the things involved in making the transition to a successful supervisor. You can benefit from expressing your views and comparing them with those of the author.

CASE #1

CASE #1:
WHO WILL SURVIVE?

> Please assume that Joe and Mary are equally qualified to assume the role of supervisor in the same department. Further assume they adopt different attitudes toward their new challenge. Which one, in your opinion, stands the best chance of surviving after six months?

Joe received news of his promotion by throwing a party. The following day he made a list of do's and don'ts he would follow. Joe figured he had worked under enough supervisors to know what to do. He would model his behavior on what he had learned from observation. Why bother to study techniques and principles in advance? Why get needlessly uptight by too much preparation. Joe believes personality and good common sense is all that is needed. His strategy will be to set a good example by personally working hard, staying close to the group and doing a lot of listening and concentrate on building good relationships in all directions. Joe has complete confidence in his ability to succeed.

Mary was delighted with the announcement of her promotion. She decided to use the two week period to prepare for her new responsibilities. She quickly found some good books on supervision and started to make a list of recommended techniques to follow. How to demonstrate authority? When to delegate? What changes in behavior would be required, etc.? Mary accepted the premise that she had much to learn about becoming a successful supervisor. Although she believes in herself, she does not have Joe's level of confidence. Mary has decided on the following strategy. Although she intends to remain friendly and upbeat, she will slowly pull back from too much personal contact with former fellow-employees. She feels this will be necessary to demonstrate her authority. Next she will concentrate on creating a good working environment so that workers are more relaxed. Everything will be planned and orderly. Everyone will know where he/she stands and what is expected.

Which individual has the better chance of survival? Will Joe with his upbeat, confident approach do a better job than Mary with her more scientific attitude? Or will Mary, with her less confident but more deliberate strategy survive over Joe? Check the appropriate box below and compare your decision with that of the author on page 68.

☐ Joe will survive.

☐ Mary will survive.

☐ Both Joe and Mary will survive.

Supervisors are *in-charge* people. As leaders, they utilize their sources of power in sensitive but effective ways. When you assume your role as a supervisor-leader, you have three sources of power from which to tap.

First, you have *knowledge power* because of what you know about the department you lead. In most cases, you *know more* than those who work for you. When you teach them what you know, you make the best use of your knowledge power.

Second, you gain power from the role you occupy. Just being the supervisor gives you authority which you must use gently and wisely.

Third, you have *personality power.* You can persuade or motivate others through your positive attitude, friendly manner, patience and other personal characteristics.

Although you must be sensitive in the way you use your power (do not let your new position go to your head), properly used, the three sources of power can help you become the kind of supervisor you want to be.

VITAL MESSAGE AHEAD

CONVERT TO A STRONGER IMAGE

It is important that a new supervisor learns to communicate a *take charge* image. She or he must let everyone know (co-workers and superiors) that things are under control—that decisions are being made and that the role of supervisor is comfortable. All of this must be accomplished without giving an impression that the new position has gone to the individual's head. It must be a natural transition.

Why is a stronger image necessary? Among other reasons, your employees want you to be a leader. They will produce more if they know they are part of a cohesive group with established standards. In contrast, a *weak* supervisor will cause employees to be confused and unproductive.

How do you communicate a stronger image? Here are some suggestions. Place a check in the square if you agree.

☐ *Improve your appearance.* Don't overdo it, but look the part. Dress for success.

☐ *Make decisive decisions.* In making decisions, do it with confidence. Demonstrate you can handle decision-making.

☐ *Set a faster tempo.* Move about with more energy. Become a model of productivity.

☐ *Handle mistakes calmly.* When things go wrong, collect the facts, and develop a solution. Show your inner strength.

☐ *Share humorous incidents.* Balance your authority with a sense of humor. Help everyone have a little fun.

☐ *Demonstrate your ability to communicate with superiors.* Employees will feel more secure and produce more when they know you can represent them with superiors.

☐ *Be a positive person.* Stay in touch with members of your crew in a positive manner. Keep in mind that their positive attitudes are dependent upon yours.

ABOVE ALL—BE ORGANIZED!

Some individuals fail in the role of supervisor because they are poor organizers. Some are unable to organize themselves or their departments. They move from one activity to another without a plan. They assign work on a helter-skelter basis without giving employees a chance to finish one assignment before a second is due.

Result?

Employees feel frustrated, insecure and they do not live up to their productivity potentials.

The answer?

As a start, it is vital to set daily goals as outlined on the facing page.

SET DAILY GOALS

Planning is simply the thinking that precedes doing. Planning means setting goals and objectives for yourself and your employees that support larger organization goals received from above. Properly articulated, most employees respond to reachable departmental goals in a positive way. This is especially true when employees have been involved in the goal-setting process and participate in the excitement when objectives are reached.

Before you became a supervisor, chances are you could do your job without much serious planning. You basically react and adjust to goals that have already been agreed upon. Your supervisor probably gave them to you. As a supervisor, a daily plan that can be reviewed and implemented *before* the work day begins is essential.

Supervisors are always planning. Planning goes with the territory. Most successful supervisors operate with a daily checklist. The smart ones:

☐ Keep a list of "to do" projects that is prioritized.

☐ Use a star or other symbol to designate projects with the highest priority.

☐ Write daily goals in their personal notebooks, planners or desk calendar.

☐ Enjoy the process of drawing a line through goals as they are reached.

☐ Recognize and reward others who help reach significant departmental goals.

Use your own system! Select your own style! But supplement your long-term departmental objectives with daily goals. It will make you feel much better on your way home each day.

PART  II

WEAVING FOUR IRREPLACEABLE FUNDAMENTALS INTO YOUR STYLE

BECOMING A GOOD SUPERVISOR IS LIKE PLAYING BASEBALL

In baseball you must cover all four bases before you score a run and contribute to the success of the team. As a supervisor, there are four principles or foundations you must master to become effective and contribute to the productivity of your organization.

You must constantly remind yourself that you are the key player and those who work for you are counting on your support.

You need not be a baseball fan for the analogy to make sense.

YOU ARE UP TO BAT

COVER ALL THE BASES AND SUCCEED

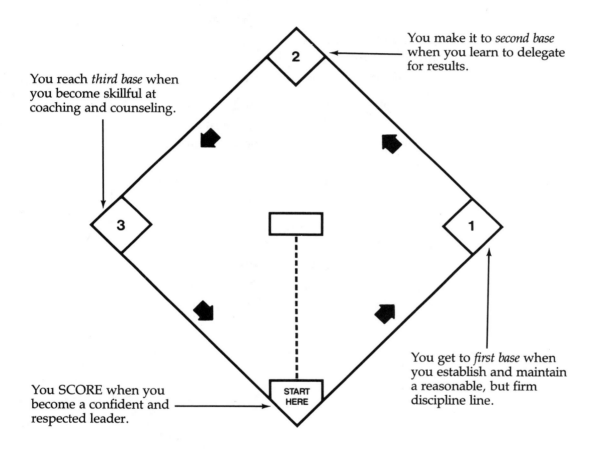

You make it to *second base* when you learn to delegate for results.

You reach *third base* when you become skillful at coaching and counseling.

You get to *first base* when you establish and maintain a reasonable, but firm discipline line.

You SCORE when you become a confident and respected leader.

In baseball you win the game when you score more runs than the opposing team. As a supervisor, you win the game when you get greater productivity from your players.

Establishing and maintaining fair, open and healthy relationships with all employees is the key to good supervision. This includes the establishment of an authority or *discipline line.* This line is a well-defined, well-communicated set of behavior standards that you expect all employees to maintain. It tells an employee what is expected and what is not permitted.

Most employees enjoy working in an environment that has high but achievable standards. They feel more secure about their jobs when their supervisor is an ''in-charge'' person who does not permit one employee to get by with recognized violations.

It is important to set a reasonable and *consistent* discipline line. As you learn to do this, keep in mind that there is nothing incompatible about showing compassion and maintaining high standards at the same time.

TIPS ON GETTING TO FIRST BASE

DEMONSTRATE YOUR AUTHORITY AND STYLE

To reach first base you must demonstrate you are in charge and know what you are doing. You need to establish a style of your own. As you do this, give your team time to adjust. You are more interested in long-term, sustainable productivity than immediate results that may not last. This means the establishment of a sound working relationship with your employees.

In making your transition, consider these tips.

1. Set high (but attainable) standards at the outset. The lower your standards at the beginning, the more difficult it will be to improve productivity later.

2. Make an effort to etablish a good relationship with each employee on an individual basis as soon as practicable. This means working to get to know each employee personally and letting them know you care. It is not a sign of weakness to show understanding. You can be a sensitive supervisor and still be tough.

3. Quickly counsel those who are not meeting your standards so they have no doubts about what is expected.

4. Keep in mind that a few important standards (or rules) are better than a list of complicated directions. Do not be a picky supervisor. Instead, set basic terms that all understand and can attain.

> **Nothing undermines your authority faster than playing favorites. Employees need to be treated equally—especially if some are personal friends.**

IT IS NOT BUSINESS AS USUAL

In order to remain competitive in a difficult environment, most organizations are streamlining their operations. This often means:

- Fewer employees to meet the same or higher productivity standards.

- More on-the-job training to help employees reach higher personal productivity.

- Tighter time schedules.

Achieving such goals throws more responsibility on the shoulders of front-line supervisors. In other words, supervisors are expected to operate in a leaner, more efficient way that will result in higher productivity. On top of this, higher levels of quality will also be expected.

Some people, especially executives, call this running a "tight ship." This does not mean that the demands on employees will be excessive. It does not mean employees will become rebellious or unhappy. Just the opposite is often true because employees like to reach goals, perform efficiently and belong to an organization that can win in tough times.

Are you prepared, as a supervisor, to accept this higher tempo of productivity? The exercise on the opposite page will help you find out.

TIGHT SHIP EXERCISE

This exercise is designed to start the process of deciding just how prepared you are to run a tight ship.

	Yes	No	Not Sure
1. Can you keep strict control over your employees without stifling their self-motivation?	☐	☐	☐
2. Can you quickly spot and correct unacceptable behavior in a subordinate without becoming upset yourself?	☐	☐	☐
3. Do you consider it a compliment when someone says you run a tight ship?	☐	☐	☐
4. Can you spot a problem in its infancy and make a correction before it grows into a major problem?	☐	☐	☐
5. Can you keep discipline among your employees without becoming heavy-handed?	☐	☐	☐
6. Can you prove that there is less employee theft in your department than there is in similar sections?	☐	☐	☐
7. Have you set up the right kind of financial reporting (systems) so you can spot trends quickly when corrections are easier?	☐	☐	☐
8. Do you enjoy spending time analyzing financial reports?	☐	☐	☐
9. Can you approach a sensitive, problem-employee in such a way that she or he makes a behavioral change while respecting you for helping?	☐	☐	☐
10. Can you run a tight ship without being so picky that employees consider you a fuddy-duddy instead of a good manager?	☐	☐	☐
TOTAL	☐	☐	☐

Seven or more ''yes'' answers indicates you may have your operation under proper control. Seven or more ''no'' or ''not sure'' answers suggests you may have problems running a lean, productive department.

SETTING THE <u>RIGHT</u> DISCIPLINE LINE

As you become a supervisor you must draw a line of discipline that employees understand. The establishment of a values framework will allow your employees to operate securely. Supervisors must set discipline lines based upon their own, special work environment and individual style.

CASE #2

CASE #2:
WHICH STRATEGY SHOULD HENRY USE?

Although sensitive to the needs of fellow-workers, Henry has always set higher standards for himself. He is never late, seldom absent and, once on the job, all business. Henry attributes his work style to his upbringing and religious training. Henry is respected more by management than fellow employees.

Yesterday Henry was promoted to supervisor of his own department. When informed of the promotion, Henry's superiors told him: ''You were selected because we think you can put some discipline back into the department. It won't be easy, but we have faith in you, Henry.''

Last night Henry sat down and developed three different strategies to consider. Which one would you recommend Henry employ?

Strategy 1   Set a good example and give employees time to adjust to it.

Strategy 2   Call a departmental meeting and, in a low-key manner, explain the mission you have been given by your superiors. Explain that the higher standards you will impose will not only protect their jobs in the future but will give them more pride in what they are doing now. Tell them you will be tough but fair.

Strategy 3   Do the same as strategy 2 but on an individual counseling basis. Call in each person and explain the changes that will be made and why.

Write out your answer below.

I would recommend that Henry employ strategy _____ for the following reasons.

_____

_____

_____

Compare your answer with that of the author on page 68.

YOU MAKE IT TO SECOND BASE WHEN YOU <u>DELEGATE</u>

Delegating is the assignment of tasks and responsibilities to help employees make their best contribution to the overall productivity of your department. When you delegate you become a teacher. You tell an employee how to perform a new task effectively, show how it is done, and then ask that he or she demonstrate the task that has been learned. Delegating takes time, patience and follow-up to insure it is done right.

A supervisor must learn how to evenly distribute tasks, tap the special creativity of each individual, and, when appropriate, rotate responsibilities among different employees. Proper delegation keeps employees motivated, increases productivity, and frees the supervisor to perform more important activities.

THE CONTRIBUTIONS OF OTHERS MAKE YOU A GOOD SUPERVISOR

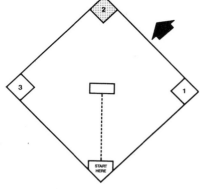

After setting a fair, consistent, discipline line, the next big lesson is that you cannot do all the work yourself. You must delegate, and allow others to have responsibility to complete tasks that meet the expectations of your organization. This means that intelligent delegation is more important than the actual work you do yourself. Building good relationships with employees helps motivate them to do the work that needs to be done. It is great for employees to like you; but respect is more important. These tips will help you meet the challenge of getting to second base. Place a check in each square as you go through the list.

☐ Nothing builds respect better than demonstrating to employees that you know what you are doing. Knowledge gives you power, and when you share it, you earn respect. Teach those who work for you everything you know to help them become more efficient.

☐ Set a good example. It is smart to pitch in and work from time to time to demonstrate your compentency. But don't overdo it. Your skills are more valuable as a supervisor than a worker.

☐ Create a relaxed but efficient working climate. People make mistakes and produce less when supervision is too close and constant. People should be able to enjoy their work within your discipline line.

☐ Circulate and communicate. Give your employees every opportunity to do a good job and when they do, follow up with compliments. Give credit freely when it is due.

☐ Keep an open door policy. That is, be accessible to employees. Welcome their suggestions and complaints. If you set a discipline line that is too tight you will destroy the environment employees need in order to produce at an optimum level.

When Molly was only twenty years of age, she became an instant supervisor without training. Although she was capable, enthusiastic, and did many things well, instead of delegating work Molly tried to do too much herself. As a result, she suffered burnout and decided that supervision was not for her. Later, at age twenty-five (after taking a course in beginning management), Molly had a second opportunity to be a supervisor. Realizing that she would be rated on what her employees did (productivity) more than what she did herself, she delegated as much as possible so she would have extra time to build good relationships, communicate, and plan. Today, at thirty-five, Molly is a successful vice-president and still growing.

HOW TO DELEGATE

Quality delegation takes planning. You must analyze all of the tasks that need to be performed *before* you start the process. Haphazard delegation can do as much harm as good.

HOW TO DELEGATE: STEPS TO TAKE

A supervisor who learns to delegate effectively achieves two goals at the same time. First, more time is available to plan, organize and maintain relationships with other employees and co-workers. Second, employees become more versatile and valuable as they learn new tasks.

Below are ten typical steps in the delegating process. As you check the list, assume you have been working extra hours and need to turn over tasks you have been doing.

☐ **Step 1** Analyze your tasks and identify one you feel will provide you with additional freedom as well as benefiting the employee to whom you assign the responsibility.

☐ **Step 2** Select the most logical individual for the task you identify and delegate it. Be careful not to overload one employee.

☐ **Step 3** Instruct the individual selected how to perform the task. Do this in detail by both explaining and demonstrating. Explain why the task is important to the total operation.

☐ **Step 4** Solicit feedback to insure the employee is prepared to assume the new responsibility. Provide opportunities for the employee to ask questions.

☐ **Step 5** Allow the employee you selected the freedom to practice the new assignment for a few days. Over-supervision can kill motivation.

☐ **Step 6** Follow up in a positive manner. When deserved, compliment the employee. If improvements are required, go through the instructional process a second time.

☐ **Step 7** Consider the rotation of tasks. Done properly, employees learn more and boredom is less likely. Also, an objective productivity comparison is possible among employees.

☐ **Step 8** Delegate those assignments that prepare employees to take over in the absence of others—including yourself.

☐ **Step 9** Give everyone an opportunity to contribute. Solicit employee ideas. Utilize their special talents and abilities.

☐ **Step 10** Discuss new assignments and rotation plans with the entire group to obtain feedback and generate enthusiasm.

If you are a sports fan, you know the primary job of a coach is to build a cohesive team. When everyone works together the team is more likely to win. Personality conflicts can destroy a team. They can also destroy productivity in a department. A supervisor is a coach. She or he must keep harmony among workers to insure productivity and win the game. The best way to do this is through good communciation and counseling.

GETTING TO THIRD BASE →

Counseling is sitting down in a private setting for an open discussion with an employee. Sometimes it is to pay a sincere compliment; sometimes it is to solve a problem that is hurting productivity; sometimes it is because an employee violated your discipline line and you need to talk about improvement in behavior. There are many counseling skills. One of the most important ones is being a good listener. This will help you find the *real* problem, and then help the employee make a mutually rewarding decision. There is no magic to good counseling. Anyone can do it.

BECOME AN EFFECTIVE COUNSELOR

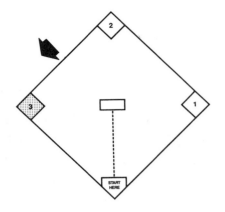

We communicate on several levels from individual to large groups. We also communicate both formally and informally. When you become a supervisor, communication of all types, at all levels, takes on new importance.

Communicating one-to-one, in private, is called counseling or interviewing. Once you become a supervisor you will discover counseling is one of the best "tools" you possess. Until you understand what counseling can do for you, it will be difficult to get to third base.

Below are ten situations. Seven call for counseling by the supervisor. *Three do not*. Check the three that require no counseling. Check your answers with those given at the bottom of the page.

☐ 1. When an employee violates your standards.

☐ 2. When an employee is consistently late or absent.

☐ 3. When you disagree with an employee's lifestyle.

☐ 4. When an employee's productivity is down.

☐ 5. When one employee behaves in such a way that the productivity of others is negatively affected.

☐ 6. When you are upset.

☐ 7. When two employees have a conflict that is becoming public.

☐ 8. When you dislike the personality of an employee.

☐ 9. When you want to compliment an individual.

☐ 10. When you want to delegate a new task.

If productivity drops in a department, action needs be taken quickly. Time normally will not solve problems that need to be addressed. Often action can take the form of counseling—either individual or group, or both.

Answers to exercise 3, 6, 8

To be an effective supervisor you need to know how to *create* and maintain relationships with members of your staff. Good relationships are created when you:

- Provide clear, complete instructions.

- Let employees know how they are doing.

- Give credit when credit is due.

- Involve people in decisions.

- Remain accessible.

THE BEST WAY TO MAINTAIN A RELATIONSHIP IS THROUGH FREQUENT COMMUNICATIONS.

CASE #3

CASE #3:
WILL MRT COUNSELING WORK?

Kathy learned about MRT counseling last week. As she understands it, the idea is to sit down with a problem employee and discuss rewards she can provide for that employee, as well as rewards that that employee can provide for her. The technique is based on The Mutual Reward Theory (MRT) which states that a relationship between two people can be enhanced when there is a satisfactory exchange of rewards between them. When the exchange is considered balanced, both parties will come out ahead.

Kathy has been having trouble with George for over a month. In desperation, she decides to call him into her office and openly discuss the situation to see if the Mutual Reward Theory can be applied. Her hope is that she can give him what he wants in exchange for a better attitude on his part.

Kathy starts the counseling session by complimenting George on his consistent productivity and asking him to suggest any rewards she is not providing that are within her capacity to provide. She informs George that she will, in turn, suggest three rewards she would like to receive from him.

Here are George's suggestions:
1. More opportunity to learn.
2. More recognition.
3. Less supervision by Kathy.

Kathy in turn asks for the following:
1. Continued high productivity.
2. More cooperation with co-workers.
3. Less hostility toward herself.

George and Kathy spend thirty minutes discussing the rewards each wants and how the other could provide them. George admits that he could be more cooperative; Kathy admits that she can provide George more opportunity to learn, and they discuss a number of ways this can be accomplished.

Will this kind of MRT counseling work for Kathy? Will it improve the relationship between Kathy and George on a permanent basis? Write your answer in the space below and compare with that of the author on page 68.

_____

_____

_____

VIEW YOURSELF AS A COACH

Counseling is when you help an employee solve a
personal problem that is lowering his or her productivity.
In most cases problems are solved because you
understand how to be a good listener. Employees often
discuss solutions they did not know existed until
someone listened to their problem and asked meaningful
questions.

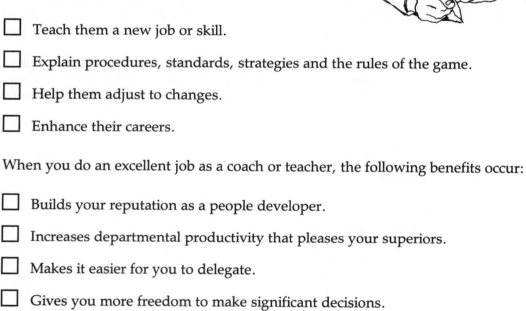

Coaching is when you help people win as individuals
so the department (team) can also win. You help
your employees win when you:

☐ Teach them a new job or skill.

☐ Explain procedures, standards, strategies and the rules of the game.

☐ Help them adjust to changes.

☐ Enhance their careers.

When you do an excellent job as a coach or teacher, the following benefits occur:

☐ Builds your reputation as a people developer.

☐ Increases departmental productivity that pleases your superiors.

☐ Makes it easier for you to delegate.

☐ Gives you more freedom to make significant decisions.

It is through good coaching techniques that winning teams are developed on
athletic fields and in business offices. Many people claim that it is smart for a new
supervisor to use her or his favorite coach as a model to develop a productivity
team in the workplace.

CASE #4

CASE #4:
CAN SYLVIA KEEP HER JOB AS A SUPERVISOR?

Sylvia, without sensing it, has been spending too much time on budget and administrative reports and not enough time communicating with her ten employees. As a result, morale is low, productivity is down and two good employees are thinking about submitting their resignations. Everyone feels frustrated and unappreciated. The situation is so bad that Sylvia's boss called her into his office and informed her: ''Sylvia, you have committed a cardinal sin by neglecting your employees in favor of other responsibilities. Instead of delegating some of your work in order to free yourself, you locked yourself in your office and allowed things to fall apart outside. You could have great potential as a manager, but not until you learn to balance people activities with job tasks. You cannot have high productivity with low communication. All of your employees feel you have been taking them for granted. A few have even talked to me about it. Your job as supervisor is in jeopardy. Be in my office at ten o'clock tomorrow with a plan to restore morale and productivity within ten days.''

What are Sylvia's chances of coming up with a plan that will turn things around?

Please check the appropriate box below and write out the reasons for your choice.

☐	☐	☐	☐
Excellent	Good	Long Shot	Too Late

_____

_____

_____

Turn to page 68 to compare your answer with that of the author.

To be highly effective as a supervisor you will want to put more leadership into your style. Everyone likes to work for a supervisor who keeps them motivated and headed in the right direction. Just like baseball players build loyalty toward coaches that lead them to victory, employees like supervisors who lead them to greater achievements.

Leadership means stepping out in front of others with new, workable ideas that save money and create greater productivity. Leadership means creating *followers* — employees who respect you to the point they would like to follow you when you earn your next promotion. Becoming a supervisor is the best possible way to learn and practice leadership skills.

GETTING HOME SAFELY

BECOME A
GOOD LEADER

Your job as a supervisor is to establish departmental goals and then lead your people to achieve them. Keeping good records and insuring that everyone stays busy is more management than leadership. Another way of saying it is that managing is the protection of what is already in place. Leadership, on the other hand, is reaching for new heights. Managers keep things the way they are to avoid trouble. Leaders take prudent risks to gain greater productivity. *YOU WANT TO BE A GOOD MANAGER, BUT YOU ALSO WANT TO BE A LEADER.*

To become both—and get home safely—consider these tips:

First, be a good manager. Insure your operation is conforming to your organization's standards. Watch details. Get reports in on time. Achieve the good feeling that comes from having everything under control.

Next, become a positive influence. Set new goals and motivate others to reach them. Stay positive. Keep things stirred up. Don't permit employees to become bored.

Help your people reach their goals. Help them feel better about themselves. Provide the rewards and recognition they deserve. The better they feel about themselves, the more they will produce.

Now and then establish your authority. Employees need to be reminded that a discipline line exists. One way to demonstrate your authority is to make decisive, difficult decisions. Another is to counsel disruptive employees and expect continued improvements in productivity.

Share good news. Keep the bad news in perspective. Look for positive things to talk about, including individual and group achievements. Make everyone feel that they are on a winning team.

LEADERSHIP CHARACTERISTICS

As you view yourself as a manager/leader, keep in mind that most leaders develop these characteristics. Please check those that you feel you already possess.

- ☐ Communicate sense of being in charge.

- ☐ Convert employees into followers.

- ☐ Strong track records on decision-making.

- ☐ Prudent risk takers.

- ☐ Articulate an inspiring mission.

- ☐ Generate a feeling of pride in followers.

- ☐ Create active tempo.

- ☐ Highly energetic.

- ☐ Stand firm on principle.

- ☐ Turn a department into a team.
  (See more on this on facing page.)

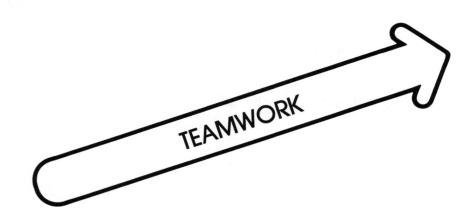

LEADERS BUILD WINNING TEAMS

Excellent managers in all types of organizations often seem content with how their group performs without trying to turn their group into a team. This may occur because they are satisfied with current productivity or have not considered what *could* be accomplished with a team approach. They refuse to accept that other managers doing similar tasks with the same technology are able to increase productivity by establishing a climate where people reach closer to their potentials and consider themselves as part of a team.

Team building is a little like baseball. The leader (coach) has the responsibility of selecting players, coordinating efforts, and, where possible, winning the game.

- Players must be committed to helping the team.

- Communication, trust and mutual support is a must.

- A reward system must be established.

- A game plan must be accepted.

ESTABLISH A
PRODUCTIVITY GOAL

Management By Objectives is a system whereby supervisors submit their goals to higher management, to be integrated with the organization's goals. Supervisors are rewarded when their goals are achieved or surpassed.

Your organization may not use this approach. If it does not, create your own goals (plans) on a weekly, monthly, and annual basis.

Those who set goals are usually more motivated to reach them. Even if management does not know about your goals (and does not hold you accountable for reaching them) you will benefit from having them.

GOALS AHEAD

Most people are goal-oriented. They like to be headed in a positive direction that will provide satisfaction.

PROVIDE DIRECTION!

Everybody likes to be on a winning team. In your organization, your department is a team that can win only if it reaches predetermined goals. *IT IS YOUR RESPONSIBILITY AS SUPERVISOR TO HELP ESTABLISH SUCH GOALS AND THEN MOTIVATE YOUR PEOPLE TO REACH THEM.*

Following are ten suggestions on how to motivate employees to reach a goal. Three are unacceptable because they will probably do more harm than good. Place a check in the squares opposite those that are counter-productive, and then compare your answers with those below.

☐   1. Involve employees in the goal-setting process.

☐   2. Make it easy for employees to motivate themselves by creating a relaxed and predictable working climate.

☐   3. At meetings, lay down the law. Tell everyone you are the boss, and things are to be done your way.

☐   4. Give employees credit when it is earned.

☐   5. Circulate regularly and listen in order to discover the kind of rewards you can provide to improve productivity.

☐   6. Act disappointed with everyone's performance as a method to get people to work harder.

☐   7. Ask for suggestions from employees on how productivity can be improved.

☐   8. Tell everyone that unless productivity improves their jobs are on the line.

☐   9. Have a positive counseling session with each employee on a regular basis. Listen to complaints, and, when possible, make adjustments to resolve the issue.

☐   10. Through your own positive attitude create a more lively and happy work environment.

It is important that each member of a team share in success. Communication is the only way this can happen.

Answers to exercise 3, 6, 8

SUMMARY—PART II

Success as a *beginning* supervisor results from following some practical principles and techniques. Although you may learn many useful management theories later, practicing the four fundamentals in this book is what you need to do to get started.

Review the four basic steps on the facing page.

PROVE YOU HAVE THE FOUR FOUNDATIONS DOWN PAT

In the weeks ahead, keep the comparison between baseball and good supervision in your mind. Make a serious attempt to weave all four foundations (bases) into your style. To help you do this, please write the missing word in each of the following sentences.

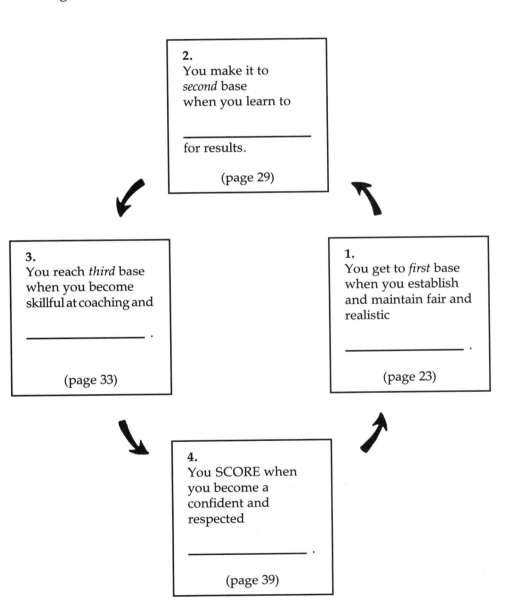

2.
You make it to *second* base when you learn to

_____

for results.

(page 29)

3.
You reach *third* base when you become skillful at coaching and

_____ .

(page 33)

1.
You get to *first* base when you establish and maintain fair and realistic

_____ .

(page 23)

4.
You SCORE when you become a confident and respected

_____ .

(page 39)

PART III

DEALING WITH SPECIAL PROBLEMS

WHEN YOU BECOME A SUPERVISOR STAYING UPBEAT GOES WITH THE TERRITORY

NEGATIVE SUPERVISORS DON'T HANG AROUND LONG

ELIMINATING PERSONAL DOWN PERIODS

It is not always easy to be positive. The responsibilities of being a supervisor are often great and they can, without realizing it, turn you negative. The truth is, that when you are positive, productivity is up; but when you become negative, productivity drops. So your challenge is to remain positive even if those around you are not.

The exercise below assumes three things: (1) You are generally a positive, upbeat person. (2) There are certain things you can do to remain positive. (3) Being aware of these activities will assist you in the elimination of down periods. After reading the list select the three that will do the most for you.

- ☐ Engage in physical exercise of some sort.
- ☐ Give yourself more attainable goals.
- ☐ Try to take life less seriously.
- ☐ Share your positive attitude with others.
- ☐ Take more week-end or ''mini'' vacations.
- ☐ Maintain a better balance between work and leisure.
- ☐ Improve your grooming.
- ☐ Do more to help others.
- ☐ Talk with a more experienced manager whom you respect to learn how to eliminate down periods.

Others:

_____

_____

_____

Gilbert is an outstanding producer, but he has a short fuse that often gets him into trouble. Maria is an excellent member of the department, but now and then she has a down period that requires great tolerance from her supervisor and co-workers. Cray makes a buddy out of all of his co-workers but becomes upset when they prefer not to include him in their activities.

Q. With such characteristics can Gilbert, Maria and Cray become successful supervisors?

A. Yes, but only if they can break those habits described above.

DANGER AHEAD

It is possible to tolerate such behavior as an employee but it could spell disaster should the same behavior surface as a supervisor.

After you hold down your job as supervisor for about three months, you will start to feel comfortable with your new role. However, you may need to change some habits before this happens.

If you are prone to make any of the mistakes listed on the following page, start to make corrections immediately or you will have trouble as a supervisor.

SIX UNFORGIVABLE MISTAKES

1. Treating individuals unequally because of sex, culture, age, educational background, etc. Each employee is unique and should receive the same consideration as any other.

2. Not keeping a trust with an employee. The fastest way to destroy a relationship is to make a promise and then break it.

3. Blowing hot and cold. Consistency is essential when managing. If you are positive one day and down the next, employees will not know how to react. Respect will disappear.

4. Failure to follow basic company policies and procedures. As a first-line supervisor, you must handle your relationship with each employee in a fair and legal manner. This may mean, for example, establishment of an improvement plan before you ask for approval to terminate an employee.

5. Losing your cool in front of others. Everyone reaches his/her threshold of tolerance on occasion; but, as a supervisor, your need to keep your temper in check. Blowing up can destroy relationships.

6. Engaging in a personal relationship with someone you supervise. When you become a supervisor, you change your role. It is poor policy to be in charge of a person during the day and personally involved with her or him after work.

In as few words as possible, rewrite the six unforgivable mistakes in your own words.

1. _____

2. _____

3. _____

4. _____

5. _____

6. _____

MOVING UP IN THE SAME DEPARTMENT IS A SPECIAL CHALLENGE. NOT EVERYONE IS COMFORTABLE MANAGING FORMER PEERS.

TRANSITION TIPS

- Stay warm and friendly but slowly back away. You cannot be a buddy and a supervisor at the same time.

- Do not permit those who were co-workers yesterday to intimidate you today. If you play favorites you are in trouble.

- Do what you can to make everyone's job better than before you became supervisor. Do not make the same mistakes your boss made when you were an employee.

- Demonstrate to your previous co-workers that you are knowledgeable by teaching them in a sensitive manner new skills that will make their jobs easier.

- Seek more assistance from your superior in making your transition. Ask for suggestions. Be a good listener.

- Give previous co-workers credit when due.

PROVIDE REINFORCEMENT

Employees like to know how they are doing. Take a few minutes every now and then to let your people know you appreciate their dependability and the contribution they are making. Many capable employees resign because superiors take them for granted.

You are only as good as the people who work for you. Make sure your employees regularly receive the reinforcement they need.

All supervisors must occasionally deal with a difficult employee. Some employees are consistently late or absent from work—others create false rumors that impact on the productivity of workers—still others fail to follow safety rules or make mistakes that need to be corrected. In extreme cases, problem employees carry hostility toward another employee or his or her supervisor.

How you deal with such employees and convert them into team members is a critical part of your job. The suggestions on the following pages are designed to provide you with the help you may need.

THE PROBLEM EMPLOYEE

REACTING TO THE PROBLEM EMPLOYEE

Below are ten ways to react to an employee who is demanding, hostile and disruptive. *Three are acceptable forms of behavior.* Place a check in the box opposite those you feel are appropriate behavior for a supervisor. Then match your answers with those at the bottom of the page. Remember, we are talking about your intial reaction—not action that might be taken later.

☐   1. Stay cool. Let the employee express anger without an immediate reaction on your part.

☐   2. Let the employee know that you consider him or her to be a problem.

☐   3. Challenge the employee with a firm countenance.

☐   4. Consider the employee as objectively as possible and refuse to take things personally.

☐   5. Avoid the problem. Time will solve it.

☐   6. Become distant and non-communicative.

☐   7. Challenge the employee to stop giving you a problem.

☐   8. Act uninterested and ignore the situation.

☐   9. Get angry and give back the kind of behavior you receive.

☐ 10. In a calm manner say: ''Let's talk in my office.''

> **Firm, friendly and fair are the key words in maintaining your discipline line. But when a difficult situation arises, it is time to use your counseling skills.**

Answers to exercise 1, 4, 10

Throughout this book you have learned that becoming a successful supervisor is a combination of many personal characteristics (positive attitude, personal confidence, patience, etc.) and the application of many tested skills and techniques (delegating, counseling, restoring relationships, etc.).

CAN YOU PUT ALL OF THESE REQUIREMENTS TOGETHER?

Of course you can—especially if you don't try to do everything at once! Keep in mind that after all is said and done, the key to your success as a supervisor is how well you achieve improved productivity.

If your department is regularly recognized for higher productivity than similar departments, your superiors will recognize this and you will be in a good position for future advancement.

Achieving greater productivity is a *human challenge.* As a supervisor, it is not what you can accomplish by doing tasks yourself, but the quality of the working relationships you build with the employees *who do the work for you.*

HOW TO ACHIEVE GREATER PRODUCTIVITY

DEVELOP YOUR HUMAN SKILLS

As an employee, your productivity was measured and compared with your co-workers. Your superior normally did this through some kind of formal appraisal. Your promotion may have depended on these appraisals.

When you become a supervisor, you are measured by the productivity of your department or section. This means your future depends on how well your crew performs. If you employ the human skills that motivate your staff to produce more, you will be recognized for doing a good job. If the opposite happens, your job may be in jeopardy.

It helps to contribute to productivity by doing a small amount of work yourself. This also helps to set the work pace. If you do too much yourself, however, your people may not get the supervision that will allow them to produce more.

To test your understanding, please answer the following true and false questions. The correct answers are given below.

True   *False*

_____ _____ 1. Nothing should receive higher priority than helping an employee reach his or her productivity potential.

_____ _____ 2. A drop in productivity by a reliable employee need not be dealt with immediately as it might cause resentment.

_____ _____ 3. Employees will often produce more for one supervisor than for another.

_____ _____ 4. A disruptive employee who reduces the productivity of co-workers must be dealt with immediately.

_____ _____ 5. Some employees with modest personal productivity can help the productivity of others so much that they are highly regarded by supervisors.

_____ _____ 6. Most employees have higher productivity potential than they realize.

_____ _____ 7. Generally speaking, the more employees produce, the better they feel about themselves.

_____ _____ 8. Human skills are easier to learn than technical skills.

_____ _____ 9. A think-smart supervisor can do less personally and still have the highest producing department.

_____ _____ 10. A "golden" employee is one who produces at a high level, and also contributes measurably to the productivity of co-workers.

Answers to exercise:
1. T 2. F 3. T 4. T 5. T 6. T 7. T 8. F 9. T 10. T

KEEPING SUPERIORS HAPPY

When you become a supervisor it is important not only to keep your employees happy and productive, it is also important to make sure that good relationships are maintained with your superiors. As mentioned earlier, you are the ''buffer'' and must be concerned with relationships in both directions.

Here are three suggestions to assist you in developing and maintaining a healthy, open relationship with *your* boss.

1. Tie your departmental goals to those of the firm as a whole. This means listening to changes that come down from above and bringing your section into line. Just as there are problem employees, there are problem supervisors. Don't be one.

2. Keep your superior informed. Share the good news (it is a good idea to have your superior compliment one of your deserving employees now and then) and openly admit any misjudgments you may have made.

3. Be a good team member. As a supervisor, you will need to build good relationships with supervisors and management other than your immediate boss. In doing this, see that your superior is placed in the best possible light with others. Do this even though she or he may not give you all the recognition you feel you deserve.

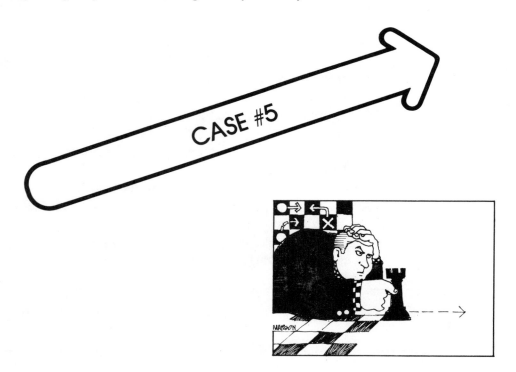

CASE #5

CASE #5:
BETWEEN A ROCK
AND A HARD PLACE

Grace did so well as a beginning supervisor for her department store that they invited her to attend an all-day management workshop. When she showed up for work the following day her superior, Mr. Adams, called her into his office and questioned her harshly about the behavior of her employees. Knowing Grace was absent, Mr. Adams had dropped by her department at closing time and found her employees playing catch with some merchandise and laughing loudly. Grace, feeling let down by her staff, told Mr. Adams it would not happen again and on the following day came down hard on everyone at an informal staff meeting. Then, after checking the sales figures, Grace discovered her group had such a great sales day—an all time record in fact—that they were simply celebrating because of their success. Mr. Adams had misinterpreted their behavior.

How, in your opinion, should Grace handle the situation? Write your answer below and compare with that of the author on page 68.

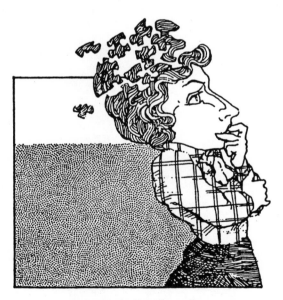

**GRACE PUTTING THE
PIECES TOGETHER**

REPAIRING RELATIONSHIPS

In becoming a successful supervisor, you will make your share of human relations mistakes. This is inevitable because your personnel responsibilities will be different. You will be exploring new human relations territory.

If you permit these mistakes to go unattended you may turn out to be the victim. This can happen when employees become offended and cut back on their personal productivity, start rumors, etc. You did not intend to damage a relationship, but you become the victim anyway. To avoid this, you may wish to consider the following:

1. Apologize by saying you are still learning the ropes.

2. Engage in some personal counseling with the injured parties so that they can get anything bothering them out in the open. Communication is not only the best way to restore a relationship, often it is the only way.

3. Without showing any favoritism, do something special to send the injured employee a signal that you know you made a mistake and that it won't happen again.

PROBLEM-SOLVING TECHNIQUES

Many qualified workers refuse opportunities to become supervisors because they do not want to face the problem-solving responsibilities that go with the job. Some of these individuals are not aware that there are proven techniques to help them make good decisions. These skills can be learned.

For example, it is helpful to divide problems into four classifications:

1. Small people-centered problems. Little requests that a supervisor can handle quickly according to acceptable practices. Sometimes, even making an exception to the rule.

2. Major people-centered problems. An employee is hostile, refuses to be a part of the team, and is a negative influence on the productivity of others. Counseling and coaching come into play. Considerable time may be involved.

3. Small job-centered problems. Little adjustments that need to be made to equipment, layout, or processes. Minimum time and effort required.

4. Major job-centered problems. Solving these problems requires time and a procedure. (1) Recognize the problem. (2) Gather data. (3) Analyze. (4) Discuss with others. (5) List options. (6) Make decision. (7) Follow up.

When a supervisor has a cool head, takes time to size up and classify a problem, and then makes a decision based on the impact the decision will have on productivity, he or she will develop a good decision-making track record.

THE STAFFING CHALLENGE

As a manager, you may or may not be deeply involved in the staffing process. Some managers have complete control over who is hired or transferred into their departments. Others must select from those sent by the Human Resources Department. Often they have refusal powers only.

Staffing includes much more than simply filling a vacancy with the best available individual. It also involves determining long-term personnel needs, orientation and training, transfers and reassignments, rotation, performance evaluation and terminations. The moment a vacancy or personnel change is in the offing, experienced managers ask themselves these questions.

- Is the function performed by the departing employee absolutely necessary?

- Could the tasks be divided among other employees?

- What skills are missing among the staff that a new employee could provide?

- What kind of person will contribute most to greater productivity?

- Is someone being trained to eventually take my job?

The goal of every manager should be to hire, develop and maintain the most cohesive and productive staff possible. Sex, race, age or handicaps cannot play a part in the selective process. The practice of first come, first hired should be avoided. Screening written applications and interviewing should be done studiously.

PULLING TOGETHER

When you think of an outstanding coach you think of someone who designs strategies so the team can win. Excellent supervisors can develop strategies. They devise plans that keep productivity at the highest possible level. To make the plan work, each member of the team must produce near his or her potential. When everyone contributes, everyone wins.

So coaches (and supervisors) motivate their players to live up to their expectations and take pride in their achievements. In doing this, they:

- Maintain a sense of humor

- Communicate and encourage involvement in the ''game plan'' of the day, week or month

- Seek a commitment to quality and performance from each individual

- Provide support for each player even when performance is not up to expectations

- See that all players are rewarded even though special recognition is given to one or two team members for unusual performance

Someone once explained that a *group* is composed of people who try to push a giant rock through uncoordinated, individual effort. The rock seldom moves. A *team* is composed of individuals who have a single goal and coordinate their efforts to achieve it. They push together and the rock quickly moves in the right direction.

In the middle of any successful team is an individual who orchestrates the efforts of each individual. This individual can be called a coach or a leader. The most common name, however, is that of a supervisor.

It is important to remember that individuals who become good first-line supervisors become candidates for middle and upper management positions. Those who demonstrate their skills in the minor leagues (supervision) are often promoted to the major leagues. In supervision, as in baseball, it is extremely important to get started on the right foot. If you weave the strategies and techniques of this book into your behavior patterns, you will be preparing yourself for a higher-paying, more challenging management role. Do not make the mistake of saying to yourself that excellent supervision is simply common sense. It is much more than that. That is why you should regularly review the skills you are learning so that you know and practice all of the competencies required to win the management game.

DEMONSTRATE YOUR PROGRESS

For each statement below, put a check under true or false.

True   *False*

1. Negotiation is not a management function.

2. *The Fifty Minute Supervisor* should be considered as Phase I of a more extended supervisory training program.

3. One way to become a successful supervisor is to do more of the actual work yourself.

4. Supervisors have less freedom than those they supervise.

5. Behavioral changes are not necessary for most people to become good supervisors.

6. Supervisors need not communicate a strong image.

7. You get to first base when you establish and maintain a fair and consistant discipline line.

8. Popularity is more important to the new supervisor than earning respect.

9. In setting a discipline line, it is better to start easy and get tough later.

10. It is easier to become a good supervisor when you are promoted within the same department.

11. Most supervisors are good at delegating.

12. Intelligent delegating takes too much time to be worthwhile.

13. Supervisors should use counseling only as a last resort.

14. Most supervisors are better at managing than leading.

15. Supervisors who stay in the background and control with a firm hand are usually the most successful.

16. Coaching and counseling are not important enough to be one of the four bases in the baseball analogy.

17. Counseling is the best technique for working with a problem employee.

18. Unlike employees, a supervisor does not have the luxury of reporting to work in a negative mood.

19. Failure to keep a promise with an employee is not an unforgiveable mistake.

20. Supervisors cannot afford to show compassion for employees.

TOTAL   **Turn page for answers.**

ANSWERS TO EXERCISE ON PAGE 65:

1. F

2. T It is possible you will be able to attend management seminars at a later date.

3. F A supervisor should *supervise*, not do actual work all the time.

4. F Supervisors have more freedom, especially if they learn how to delegate.

5. F Many behavioral changes are usually necessary.

6. F A stronger image is necessary, but, of course, it should not be done too quickly or overdone.

7. T (See page 23)

8. F

9. F Just the opposite; start out with a firm but fair line and relax to the proper point later.

10. F Just the opposite.

11. F

12. F It takes time at the beginning but releases time in the future.

13. F Counseling is a tool that can be used daily.

14. T

15. F Constant communication through circulation is required.

16. F Coaching and counseling constitute third base.

17. T

18. T If the supervisor is down, the entire crew may be.

19. F

20. F There is nothing incompatible about being compassionate and still maintaining a strong, productive discipline line.

PREPARING FOR PHASE II OF YOUR MANAGEMENT TRAINING

What you have learned from this booklet should be considered Phase I in an on-going plan of personal growth into higher management levels. Think of it as a strategy to get you off and running on the right foot. Later, perhaps sooner than you think, you may have the opportunity to attend a Phase II seminar offered by your organization. Or you can enroll in a management course at a local college on your own. One thing for certain, the progress you make in more sophisticated programs will depend upon your success with Phase I.

As you look ahead to your future in management, please keep the following in mind:

1. Nothing can take the place of a positive supervisory experience at the very beginning. Some individuals who get off to a bad start return to non-supervisory roles and never try again.

2. The more you apply the basic principles and simple techniques of this book the better your start will be.

3. Once you can handle the basics you will automatically become confident and insightful regarding more difficult management problems.

4. After you have been a supervisor for a few months, you may wish to consider completing THE MANAGEMENT DEVELOPMENT PROFILE in the new Crisp book *Rate Your Skills as a Manager.* This exercise will help you measure your progress and introduce you to some more demanding aspects of management. Contact your distributor or write Crisp Publications at 95 First Street, Los Altos, California 94022, for more information.

AUTHOR'S SUGGESTED ANSWERS TO CASES

Case #1

Who Will Survive? It is the opinion of the author that both Joe and Mary will survive, but the edge is with Mary. Joe will probably be better liked as a supervisor. Mary, however, will probably earn more respect. Joe may be too casual in learning the many sound techniques and principles every supervisor should learn.

Case #3

Which Strategy Should Henry Use? The author favors strategy two but would also follow up the group session with individual counseling to avoid any misunderstandings and improve relationships. Henry should not expect 100% compliance to his new standards quickly. He should, however, set his standards high enough to achieve the kind of productivity desired. Reachable standards are required, but employees should be given sufficient time to reach them. While doing this, Henry should also set a good example both as a supervisor and worker.

Case #3

Can Sylvia Keep Her Job As A Supervisor? It is doubtful that Sylvia can turn things around. In fact, in similar situations, many experienced managers would transfer Sylvia to a non-supervisory position until she can demonstrate she is ready to assume the full responsibility of being a supervisor. Sylvia's boss is right in saying she committed a cardinal sin. The only way a supervisor can increase or maintain productivity is to establish and nuture good relationships with all employees. Once other activities take priority, morale begins to fall and trouble starts. Restoring relationships at this point is a long shot. Once relationships have deteriorated to a certain point, rebuilding them is almost impossible.

Case #4

Will MRT Counseling Work? If both Kathy and George make a serious effort to provide one or more of the rewards wanted, but not previously provided, the chances are excellent that the relationship will improve. MRT counseling frequently works because it opens up communication and both parties accept that there is something specific to do to make improvements. Care should be taken to announce in advance that there may be some rewards (like an increase in pay) over which the supervisor does not have jurisdiction or complete control.

Case #5

Between A Rock and A Hard Place. First Grace should go to Mr. Adams and explain the reason for their behavior and stand up for them and their high productivity. Second, she should tell her staff what happened at the meeting with Mr. Adams. A supervisor's first responsibility is to go to bat for his or her staff.

NOTES

FOR OTHER FIFTY-MINUTE SELF-STUDY BOOKS
SEE THE BACK OF THIS BOOK.

NOTES

FOR OTHER FIFTY-MINUTE SELF-STUDY BOOKS
SEE THE BACK OF THIS BOOK.

NOTES

FOR OTHER FIFTY-MINUTE SELF-STUDY BOOKS
SEE THE BACK OF THIS BOOK.

NOTES

NOTES

FOR OTHER FIFTY-MINUTE SELF-STUDY BOOKS
SEE THE BACK OF THIS BOOK.

NOTES

FOR OTHER FIFTY-MINUTE SELF-STUDY BOOKS
SEE THE BACK OF THIS BOOK.

ABOUT THE FIFTY-MINUTE SERIES

We hope you enjoyed this book and found it valuable. If so, we have good news for you. This title is part of the best selling *FIFTY-MINUTE Series* of books. All other books are similar in size and identical in price. Several books are supported with a training video. These are identified by the symbol **V** next to the title.

Since the first *FIFTY-MINUTE* book appeared in 1986, more than five million copies have been sold worldwide. Each book was developed with the reader in mind. The result is a concise, high quality module written in a positive, readable self-study format.

FIFTY-MINUTE Books and Videos are available from your distributor or from Crisp Publications, Inc., 95 First Street, Los Altos, CA 94022. A free current catalog is available on request.

The complete list of *FIFTY-MINUTE Series* Books and Videos are listed on the following pages and organized by general subject area.

MANAGEMENT TRAINING (Cont.)

PERSONNEL/HUMAN RESOURCES

COMMUNICATIONS

CUSTOMER SERVICE/SALES TRAINING (CONT.)

SMALL BUSINESS/FINANCIAL PLANNING

ADULT LITERACY/BASIC LEARNING

CAREER BUILDING

To order books/videos from the FIFTY-MINUTE Series, please:

1. **CONTACT YOUR DISTRIBUTOR**

   or

2. **Write to Crisp Publications, Inc.**
   95 First Street   (415) 949-4888 - phone
   Los Altos, CA 94022   (415) 949-1610 - FAX